The Search for Wonder
in the Cradle of the World

poems by
Anthony S. Abbott

St. Andrews College Press
Laurinburg, North Carolina
2000

for Susan

This book is made possible through the *Richard Walser and Bernice Kelly Harris Fund* of the Hanes Charitable Lead Trust

Library of Congress Cataloging-in-Publication Data

Abbott, Anthony S./the search for wonder in the cradle of the world/ Anthony S. Abbott—Laurinburg, NC/St. Andrews College Press I. Abbott, Anthony S.. II. Title

St. Andrews College Press
1700 Dogwood Mile
Laurinburg, NC 28352

www.sapc.edu/sapress

Second Printing: July 2001

Acknowledgements

Theology Today: "Genesis," "Point of Light," "Dodona: Sunday Morning"

Crucible: "Fathers," "Father William," "Unburdening," "The Slow Beginning of Our Lives," "Come Lord Jesus"

N.C. Literary Review: "The Photograph: Fifty Years After"

Independence Boulevard: "Genealogy," "Once You"

Lyricist: "On the First Day of School," "One Talent Man," "Nile Journey"

Main Street Rag: "The Boy and the Purple Purse," "This Business of Graveyards"

Interim: "Coming Out"

Radix: "Raining on God"

Charlotte Poetry Review: "What Do Men Want?" "In Russia, the Grandmothers," "Election Night"

Coastal Plains Poetry: "Rings," "The Philosophers"

Asheville Poetry Review: "Aids by Transfusion," "Finders Keepers"

Cairn: "What We Have"

Pembroke Magazine: "Wherever You Are"

The Writer: "The Missing Heron"

Wellspring: "Beyond the Ceiling of Our Dreams"

Mount Olive Review: "That Which Cannot Be Done"

Yemasee: "Walking on Water"

Kent Quarterly: "Sunset on Skiff Mountain," "Under the Marble's Chiseled Skin"

"Alphabet Soup" was published in *Trapping Time Between the Branches: An Anthology from Charlotte Poets.*

Genesis

What We Have

Alphabet Soup

The Search for Wonder
in the Cradle of the World

Genesis

Genesis

For Stephen and Katy

The swinging Lord, that master maker
of cool chords, shifted in his empty
heaven and said, "I need me some music,"

So the sky was full of music
and he declared that it was good

And then the equally androgynous Lord
said to herself, I need some light
to fill the fragrant fingers of the night

So the waters shone with light
and she declared that it was good

And when the light and the music played
together the stars wept for the beauty of it
And the swinging, singing Lord said

I need me some people to praise
this thing that I have made

The Lord thought long and long about what
sort of people might be the purest praisers,
what sort of people might truly see the light

And he made man, with his cunning brain,
and he made the zebras and the elk
and the swift running antelope for man

to wonder at. And she made woman with her
imagining mind and her long, limber dancing
legs and her eyes that saw the color in the light

And when the man and woman had been crafted
The Lord declared that it was good

Then the man heard the light in the woman's eyes
And the woman saw the music in the man's mind
And the music was the silky manes of violins

And the light was like the laughter of clarinets
and the glitter of guitars. And the man and the
woman moved to the measure of the music and swayed

to the gold and amber brilliance of the light.
And they knew that the sound was neither his nor hers
nor like anything that ever was before.

And the Lord saw what they had made
And behold it was very good

Fathers

For Cathy Smith Bowers

"You're so old"
you said to me in the parking lot
after the conference ten years ago.
Angry, I turned away.
Now I'm so old it doesn't matter,
and so are you.

What matters is the truth.
What matters is these fathers
who endure long past their deaths,
long past their various leavings.

You loved yours in spite of everything,
loved him even though he burned
your clothes and lied about his name.

Mine wrote my mother letters
after their divorce,
Hundreds of them, begging, pleading
for her love. In one of them

he said that I must never know
his doubts about my birth.
I was sitting on my sister's kitchen
floor, the two of us side by side
"Holy shit," I said and laid my face
in the softness of her neck.

Later it was better. She said she'd known
his fear for years, but never believed
it true. Besides, who cared?

What fathers are or aren't
had been accomplished long before.
Still I wonder sometimes who my mother
loved the night she got me
and what prints I track in the dark lines of my unknown genes.

The Photograph: Fifty Years After

For Nancy

The boy had only wanted to see her in white,
and walk her down the aisle, there being
no father to give her away. After all, she
was his sister, and she had promised.

For years he lamented her betrayal, her eloping
with the slick piano player from Georgia,
Sea Island honeymoon and all, while he was marooned
in that yellow boarding school between cold sheets.

Now he knows better. Now, fifty years later
he knows better. He has seen the photograph,
where she sits, hair parted in the middle,
gardenias pinned above the ear, white blouse,
blue jacket, head cast down—slight hint
of shyness—eyes looking up with hope,
and a smile as young as creation's first day.

All that hope, that radiance. There she sits,
high school graduate, life before her, smiling
at the world. And why? What had she to smile
about? Youth, beauty, and a mother so drunk
they'd shipped her off to the state funny farm—
no Betty Ford clinics in those days. Stepfather
gone, vanished into the hoodlum streets of New York,
and the girl alone in the house, eighteen,
no job, no money and the landlady crying
for the rent. This smile, and for whom?

For the landlady, who relented, took the girl
into her own home, rented the empty house—
for the landlady who just happened to be
a photographer and the girl was looking for
a job, no high school picture to submit,
nothing but the clothes on her back. So what
the heck, it was the least she could do

for this girl who would go to a bar one night
and fall for the sweet fingers of the piano
player. No wonder they bolted. And the boy,
away at camp and then at the yellow school
wondering where she was, not knowing about
the mother or the rent or how hard it was
just to be a girl of eighteen with nothing
but hope and a smile and the scent of white
gardenias in her hair.

Genealogy

My sister and her husband have slipped
to the backside of the world's face.
They have leaned their hearts to the edge
of wilderness. Deer nibble from their apple
trees without fear. Rabbits with literary
names cavort freely on the unkempt grass.

In boxes on her shelf sleep pictures
of the past. On her computer screen rise
names, those Biblical begots which skip
across the centuries to Adam or the Mayflower
whichever God made first. Cousins proliferate
like crows on crossed telephone lines.

Snow falls like love lost on the elements
of time. I dig with the boots of memory.
I cut the face of the forgotten past
drawing blood. I crave the rich pain of lips
and eyes, the rough gravel of words heard,
of tears long dried in the once forgotten night.

I cast backward for mother, who must have
flipped the hearts of men with that smile,
who spent her salad years exercising my frozen
feet so I could walk, who must have sent
me something in the blood, something in the nose
or hair to keep, to love, and pass blithely along.

But the streets speak silence, and the doors
on upper Broadway and the tunnel where the train
rolled under Park Avenue to rest in Grand Central's
arms give mute testimony to memory's defeat. Only
my sister knows, and she has slipped to the back
side of the world's face, leaning her heart to
wilderness.

On the First Day of School

they sent the boy home. He had forgotten
to bring something—a form perhaps
signed by his mother. He lived nearby,
not too far to walk.

              On the way
he became frightened. His mother
would be angry with him. Maybe
she would punish him. He stood
at the front door, his hand on the handle
of the brass knocker shaped like
the head of an elephant. Shrubs grew
under the window, and it seemed to the boy
that behind these shrubs he could wait,
crouching as if invisible, until the time
when school ended.

Then he would come out as if
nothing had happened, as if nothing
had gone wrong.

              But the next day
they sent him to kindergarten.
He was, they said, not ready
for first grade.

One Talent Man

He also who had received the one talent came forward, saying,
"Master I knew you to be a hard man, reaping where you did
not sow and gathering where you did not winnow; so I was
afraid, and I went and hid your talent in the ground. Here you
have what is yours."

Matthew 25: 24-25

As a kid I had it cold. Get five make five.
The school I went to had a Latin motto:
"Poteris Modo Velis,"—You Can If You Will.
It was easy. Get three make three, and so on.

I read it in the Bible my mother gave me
for my ninth birthday. I underlined the words
in red. It was simple—except for the one
talent man. He was different. He was a slob.

He was fat—with pimples. Zits. A jerk,
a nerd, a nobody, a rotting heap of vegetation,
a stupid, useless fool. God was fair.
The kid was no good. He got what he deserved.

Now I don't know. Seriously, I don't know.
Maybe the servant got a raw deal. Maybe
he was lame or halt or blind. One talent
isn't much. Maybe he thought usury was

wrong. "You ought to have invested my money
with the bankers," the master says. Whoa!
In the Old Testament they kill people
for doing that. I see him out there at night

burying the beautiful talent in the earth,
watching the dirt slowly cover the burnished
gold. Maybe he'd shined it one last time
before he let it go. Well, it would be safe

at least, he thought. And then this master,
this God, casting him into outer darkness
and all that. And I think—this guy is me,
ME—not some pimpled slob down the block.

And the five and three talent men standing
by so smug, so satisfied, smirking at each
other like the guy in the popular song
they call sixty minute man. Thirty seconds,

is what I am. Then there's this weeping
and gnashing of teeth, and for what?
I mean, where's the grace, God, for the
poor slob who buried it in the ground?

The Boy and the Purple Purse

A nineteen-fifties spring, the city yawns,
stretches and sloughs off winter's palsied skin.
The boy is high on smoke, he scoffs at lawns.
The smell of dirt and birds is not for him.

Tonight he'll dance to Condon's Dixieland,
tomorrow Drake in Porter's Kiss Me Kate.
The Music Hall fills out his little plan,
he smiles and flicks his ashes in the grate,

then looks up just in time to see
a woman struggling toward him purse in hand
dangling from a twisted purple strand
One eye unmoored, she mumbles to her knee.

Legs marbled, pasty white start out
below a garish, checkered coat.
Fixing-him Cassandra-like, she shouts
"And what are you so goddamn happy about?"

She whomps him with the swinging purple purse
then stumbles on in conference with her thighs.
He pauses, stunned. He had not known such creatures
walked beyond his shining bright blue eyes.

Coming Out

"In short, I was afraid."

—*The Love Song of J. Alfred Prufrock*

In the long nights of the last
full moon he lay awake deep
into the fingers of the morning,
thinking, thinking of this thing

like a bird in a bramble bush
beating its wings against the tangled
boughs of fear. In the still center
he was safe. From the still center

he could watch feet and the wet
noses of deer, he could see wild
flowers and scudding clouds, a hint
of blue behind. Here it was dark.

Here he was not seen, here he could
lick his wings and wait. If blood
were asked, then let others bleed
in the silver slivers of moonlight

on the rough and untamed ground
out there. There are many ways
to die, he thought, in the whiteness
of his room under the lagging moon.

In the Chapel

It had, of course, always been holy, at least
to him, and when he returned, what shocked
was not so much the crassness—the moneychangers
in the temple and all that—but the outright air
of innocence they wore. The blond girl, laying
her head on the chair's hard back and closing
her eyes, then sweetly smiling when she woke
as if to say hello in a field of flowers, the other
next to her, darker with the pug nose and the math,
calculator working hard to fit the figures in the boxes
while the words of the sermon or the prayers, it didn't
matter which, floated high over their heads into
the beams themselves.

                They wore their sin
with such insouciance, the boys in the north aisle
huddling with their baseball caps turned backward
on their shaven heads, sneakers squeaking on the
tired stone, the hymnbooks closed, the wet words
falling like snowflakes on the winter ground,

And he, foolish among those faces, trying to sing
by heart the words of the school song, trying
to stop the quaver in his voice lest he seem
too sad here, in the dancing ruin of his faith.

Maybe he was wrong, maybe he and his had been
the same, but he held no images of play
from former years, only the flicker of the candles
and the frightening chords of the new headmaster's
holy texts which cut through the spaces of the skull-
held world into the vast reaches of eternity.

Raining on God

For Lee Whitman

> *"Do you think God gets rained on?"*
> *"It beats me, Betsy, how to answer the question. I just*
> *don't know what to say. What do you think?"*
> *"I think He gets rained on a lot. Just because it's*
> *heaven doesn't mean there's no rain."*

—Robert Coles, *The Spiritual Life of Children*

Twenty-five years ago today my daughter
went to sleep and woke—somewhere else.
Outside the forsythia had burst into
mocking yellow grandeur as it does now
in my neighbor's yard across the way.

I like to think of the sadness of God,
the rain in God's face the day his son
was crucified, God helpless as the rest
of us to pull the nails or even wipe
the stinking sweat from his son's eyes.

I don't know, Lee. All we can do
is love. The rest seems way beyond me.
I think of your Rebecca. Why her? Why me?
Why ten million Jews? Yesterday a dog
escaped its yard and chased a child

into the path of a passing pickup truck.
The day my daughter died my older son's
best friend beat his head black and blue
against the trunk of a back-yard apple tree.
Don't punish yourself. Today on the campus

huge cardboard radishes and carrots, roses
and clumps of broccoli swing in the wind
from the bare branches of trees. Japanese
tulips bud. Your Becca is beautiful beyond
any words I can make for her.

The White Dogs

To the Memory of Robert T. Stone (1940-1995)

On the day that Bob Stone died
    the white dogs came
        from over the hills beyond the sky

On the day that Bob Stone died
    his wife and daughter stood
        by the side of his bed and waited

for a change in his breathing.
    It was then that they heard
        the sound of the two Salukis—

dogs of the Pharaohs, dogs of the old gods
    and the passage to the world below
        with all its magic splendors.

The two dogs came to the open door
    of the mountain cabin
        And looked in with wide eyes.

They stood like messengers
    in their smooth coats
        with their lean and muscled legs.

They stood by the open doors and watched
    while his breathing slowed
        they waited as his breathing stopped

then flew, invisible, over the mountain pines
    with their new soul
        their angel friend who laughed

with the joy of his new freedom,
    their friend who knew in his heart
        the court of the King he loved

and now he flew to those loving arms
    born by his companions
        the white Salukis, messengers of the Lord.

Point of Light

For Susan and Kevin

We know so little. Who is to say what
truth is? When the door has been closed
and the light turned off for the night,
Who is to say what goes on in that room

we call God? Who is to say what God
thinks or knows about our pain and why
we have it. In the case of a child
we think the worst. Yesterday I thought

of my daughter who died so many
years ago, and how I talked to God
then and said, "All right, you've done
the worst and I'm still here."

And how I burned with anger, helpless
with rage, and how later she came
to my son in a dream, beautiful
and whole and grown into woman

and told him she was well, told
him not to fear. And I think of you
now in your pain and how you must
ask God every day why Jack should

hurt so much and how it is only
later we can know anything at all.
So for now, think of your courage
as a gift, and think of each small

step down the hall, each nurse's
touch, each friend's voice as God.
Think Donna and Eileen and Pat
think of the cells themselves created

like the universe from nothing
and that strange emptiness under
the pain where God starts to work—
and how he shines there, glows

in the marrow of these new bones.

What We Have

What Do Men Want?

"Drums, sweat, and tears," says *Newsweek*
Magazine, telling of wild-man weekends
in the woods and tales of missing fathers
in the sweat-house. It's not so simple.

In my fifteenth year my mother died.
Embarrassed not to cry, I tucked my head
under the sheets and feigned tears
for my older sister's eyes and ears.

In my thirtieth year on the Monday
after Easter my daughter went to bed
and never woke. Strong men carried her out.
Her arm hung down below the stretcher's

side. Dry-eyed I picked it up and put
it back. At thirty-five I struck
a boy for stealing from my son.
I spun and spun, darkly off balance,

hearing my voice, as if a stranger's,
ringing in distant ears. By forty
I learned the stepping stones of grief
and how the smallest things are joined.

Bach and the Beatles and "Amazing Grace,"
the quaking aspen leaves and sugar maples
in the fall could set me off on cue.
At fifty I fake colds instead of tears,

blowing my nose at "Thelma and Louise."
What do men want? I don't know.
The right to grieve and not be mocked,
to touch and be touched, to walk

beyond the porch steps of the soul,
to have dreams and speak them without fear.
To lie under the willow tree of love.
To seek truth in whispers not in shouts.

I like that better than drumming.

In Russia, the Grandmothers

for Rosemary Raynal

In Russia the grandmothers stand in line for bread.
All day, my friend tells me, the grandmothers stand—
waiting to buy a ticket. And then, she says, they
must take their ticket to another line, and stand
some more, until—maybe—if there's any left,
they have some bread. If the bread is gone, they go
back to the first line to get their money back.

This is crazy, I say to my friend, this standing—
these babushkas—these grandmothers with kerchiefs
on their heads—standing in line all this time.
But my friend shakes her head. They don't mind it,
she says. They talk. They laugh and they cry.
All the time they are standing in line for bread,
for shoes, for vodka, they are laughing and crying.

In the big department stores, they ride the escalators
up and down, talking and laughing and crying. They are
happy to be with their friends. They bring flowers
and they hug each other on the escalators in the big
department stories and they cry. Then they go home
to make tea for the children and the mamas and papas
who have worked all day. I am not a crying woman,

my friend says, but in Russia I cried all the time.

Richard Walking

In our white town where neighbors clip their lawns
and children ride in purple helmets off
to school, Richard walks, Richard only walks.

For years he lived in his parents' house, stately
under giant elms. They died, and he stayed on
alone, walking into town for food and Coca-Cola.

For years, he walked to town, chatted with friends
under the blue and orange Gulf sign, The house
aged, floors slanted, dishes piled in the leaking

sink. One day a salesman came, sweating
in the August sun, gave him Coca-Cola,
promised him a box of Reese's Cups

and five hundred dollars for the old place.
How Richard laughed, Richard who could
add, subtract, divide and multiply,

a regular computer, Richard who knew
the times of every train in the state.
He signed the deed and took it to his friends

at the Gulf. They got the courts to annul
the sale. The village swore to keep Richard
safe. And Richard walked, every day

he walked into the arms of his town
until one afternoon near the grocery
store a boy struck him with a lead pipe,

broke his leg, threw him to the ground
bent his arm back, stole his money, and
walked, walked away, here in our town

of swallows and wrens and red brick.
"I always did want to be on crutches,"
Richard said, "but not this way, not this."

The Philosophers

The philosophers have stopped driving—
they have returned their licenses
to the Department of Motor Vehicles
believing that it is inherently unsafe
for them to operate same. To figure out
the universe and manage stop signs
at the same time is more than their minds
can manage. I understand the problem

having failed to yield when searching
my brain for the name of the President
who followed Grover Cleveland Alexander,

having backed unceremoniously
into U.S. mailboxes while trying
to solve the most rudimentary algebraic
equation, having dipped into low shoulders
while imagining shoulders of another sort.

I sympathize. When I imagine the magnitude
of their tasks, I wonder how they manage
even to dress themselves. Einstein, they say,
had fifteen suits exactly the same color
so he would not have to stop and ponder
what to wear. And policemen in Princeton,
New Jersey, are known to have led him home
from relatively long walks.

I admire the philosophers, but I am glad
that they no longer drive. Immanuel Kant
walked every day of his entire adult life,
and the women of Königsberg, his native town,
could set their clocks by his passing.

Election Night

The last animal at the Sarajevo zoo
died today, a small brown bear who
starved to death because the keeper
could no longer feed him. It is autumn
and the leaves had fallen from the trees,
so now the snipers could see to shoot
when the man brought the bear his food.

The morning paper tells also of a doctor
who has bilked the government of thousands
by cutting the toenails of old people
in nursing homes and charging Medicaid
for major surgery.

                        Last night, in Beaufort,
South Carolina, a seaside town where people
often come to tour the Antebellum homes,
a secretary at the local college was shot
in the mouth at point blank range by someone
who stole what little cash she had for drugs.

And yet tonight, just minutes ago, before vast
and cheering throngs, our president-elect
has promised us a new beginning.

Aids by Transfusion

... we turn him into an anecdote to dine out on. Or dine in on.
But it was an experience. I will not turn him into an anecdote.
How do we fit what happened to us into life without turning it into
an anecdote with no teeth and a punch line you'll mouth over and
over for years to come.

—John Guare, *Six Degrees of Separation*

On the corner of Broadway and Sixty-Seventh Street
near the Opera with the flash of its Marc Chagall
murals, near the symphony, near the Vivian Beaumont
theatre from whose plush red seats we had just risen

a man sits huddled in a blanket, silent, his message
printed in block letters on his cardboard box.
"Aids by transfusion," it reads. "Need 64 dollars
for bus ticket to Florida." My wife bends to him.

She whispers words I cannot hear. He whispers
back. She pulls three twenties from her purse
and stuffs them, crumpled, in his groping hand.
He smiles in thanks through wounded teeth.

In the play we had just seen, a black man cons
rich New Yorkers. He pretends to be the bastard
son of Sidney Poitier. He promises them parts
in the film of Cats. He takes their money and vanishes.

My wife feeds the homeless on Friday nights
driving by their cardboard boxes under bridges
with blankets and food and sweaters for the cold.
She calls them all by name. She loves them.

"Do you think it's true, his story about AIDS?"
I ask her as we cross the street. "Does it
matter?" she snaps, and walks ahead as if
I am not there. "Wait!" I call and follow after.

This Business of Graveyards

Here on Author's Ridge Henry David Thoreau
rests next to his beloved brother John,
beside father, mother, sisters. The late
afternoon sun slants through the rich green
leaves dotting the dark stone with dancing
imps of light. Soon it will be dark. Soon
they will close the iron gates. I move quickly

from grave to grave, stone to stone, searching
for some truth from the dead. Bronson and Louisa
Alcott, dying the same year. Hawthorne, here alone
separated by the gray Atlantic from his Sophia.
Emerson, grand even in death, rests beneath
a huge uncut natural slab of white granite.

Bodies say nothing. We have so little time.
I think of the stone floor of St. Patrick's,
Dublin, where Swift lies by Stella, his own
words carved in our hearts: "Ubi Saeva Indignatio
Ulterius Cor Lacerare Nequit." He has gone
where savage indignation can lacerate his heart
no longer.

Dickinson in Amherst. "Which Dickinson?" I ask,
wandering hatless in the rain through the old
cemetery which houses hundreds by that name.
Then I see her, beneath a split trunk cedar
framed by a black wrought-iron fence. I bend
and pluck two spears of grass from near her stone.

She lies, of course, by her precious sister,
Vinnie, and it comes to me suddenly, like her
own slant of light, that they all go home
in death to dwell with those of closest blood.
Even the odd ones who stumbled through this
scurvy world bellowing "no" in blunted lines.

Overhead a bird cries. In my mind a winged
voyager starts for Yucatan or Cuernavaca.
My glasses fog in the rain, and I wipe them
with the tail of my shirt. I am rooted here,
overwhelmed by earth, sinking downward
into the sweet silence of dark.

Rings

My new friend owns many gold rings.
She shows them to me on her sleeping
porch, where she writes poems late
at night after her husband has gone

to bed. The oldest, with a single pearl,
her mother bought for her eleventh
birthday with money from the grocery
jar. She lines the others up

on the coffee table—sapphires, rubies,
emeralds (her birth stone)—given
by her husband on various occasions.
"He gives me what he can," she tells me

quietly. Her favorite, an Italian ring,
crafted by the jeweler Santamaria,
Via Condotti, Roma, in Eighteen twenty-five.
It has thirty-four perfectly cut

almondine garnets, and in the center
a huge imitation diamond made of
rock-paste quartz, which Italian women
wore to plays, leaving the real ones

safely at home. "I would give them all
away," she says. "I would give them all
for . . ." She starts to fill the silence
with a word, then pauses as if to weigh

a change of mind. "No," she says, "I would."

Finders, Keepers

losers, weepers goes the old
child's rhyme, but who knows
what it means? I didn't really

until last Sunday in the park
sitting on the stone wall
when you told me the squirrel

story, you know, about saving
Winken, Blinken, and little Nod
—whom you liked best of all

because she was so small—
so fragile—and how you took
the tiny grape skin from her

throat. "She would have died,"
you said, and then you smiled
because, of course, she didn't

and you laughed telling about
the squirrel half-way-house
where they lived protected

in a kind of wild and chattered
on your shoulder when you came
to visit. You never really lose

them, do you, after something
like that, and what you end
up finding, somehow, is yourself.

"It's the best thing I ever did,"
you said, in the park on Sunday,
and all the while it was ninety

degrees, and the stone wall hard
on the buns, which, of course,
I never even noticed.

Father William

"No one will have to die alone in fear"

—*from the AIDS Memorial Quilt*

1.

How the autumn lingers here.
Mid November, yet the red bush
outside my window still beams,
the maple in my neighbor's yard
glows gold in the morning sun.

We are old, Father William,
our bodies as shapeless
as used shoes, our brains
forgetful as the ashes
of last winter's fires.

But still the autumn lingers
and the birds perch on the wires
here, where orange turns
to rust in early evening.

2.

In the night it rains
and it seems to me in dreams
that the leaves are names
falling in multitudes—names
I saw this evening on the walls
and floor of the old gymnasium—

Michael Morgan Rainwater, Deborah Wilcox,
Sunnye Sherman, Jeremiah Denkins, Larry
Jackson Buchanan, Peter M. Mazzoni, M.D.
Brad Davis, actor; Rev. Bob Hearn, Dean
Chateauneuf, Donnie Underwood, Zack Long

3.

We are old, Father William,
the leaves fall in multitudes
and where we go it will be colder still.

In the gym the young girls say the names
in silence and hold each other's hands.
They trace the shapes of the letters
with their fingers.
Their eyes are filled with tears.

Outside the autumn lingers still
in the tumbling hours
of these fading days.

On Seeing Oliver Cromwell's Portrait
at Sidney Sussex College

Poor Oliver, not even your head is safe
which once astride your cocky, wide brimmed self
ruled two universities and a Commonwealth.
Chopped and poled by Good King Charles's men,
it stewed on gates, was wrapped and passed and then
it settled here in Cambridge all alone
its final resting place, alas, unknown
lest hideous vandals find the sacred stone.

Your portrait here in Sidney Sussex hall
Must stay all veiled when royalty comes to call.
You who conquered Ireland, proclaimed
corruption's doom, today in native Huntingdon
your kingdom's one small room, where Sunday afternoons
from one to three, an ancient guide gives tours for free.
What crimes did you commit to draw such ire?
What sins to earn such fire. How long can hatred last?

Treasure Hunt

For Karl Plank

The kingdom of heaven is like treasure hidden in a field,
which a man found and covered up; then in his joy
he goes and sells all that he has and buys that field.

Matthew 13:44

I have been thinking of this since Thursday,
the field with the treasure in it, and what
it looked like, trying to picture the guy
walking along the road beside an ordinary
field with wild flowers he doesn't even
know the name of—a guy like you or me.
He isn't out trying to find treasure,
but just walking and admiring the beauty
of the day, late September, the morning air
crisp like fresh lettuce, and he sees it
by mistake even, and he rubs his eyes
because—well, because—he's never seen
anything like this before, and his first
thought is he's either blind or crazy.
It's like, as you said, Karl, find the
hidden object in the picture. You look
and look and look and never see it, and then
one day—dum de dum—you're walking along
and boom! There it is. And you're in big
trouble, because now your whole life has
changed. Oh shit, you think. I can't do this.
I'm just an ordinary guy. I don't need
this. I know what happens to those people
that win the lottery. Who wants a million?
It's nothing but stress and taxes.

So he goes home, and carries on as if
he's just the same, but he isn't and he
never will be again. That's the joy, Karl,
and the pain, too. Because after that, the
things the world wants—the suits and cars
and even trout stuffed with crab meat—aren't
ever quite the same either. So he keeps sneaking
back to catch a glimpse of the treasure, which

he's covered up of course in case some other
guy should come along and spot it (which must
be a mistake since God says the treasure is for
everyone). And every time he gets a glimpse
his heart goes bonkers. It's so beautiful
it freaks him out. It makes him want to laugh
and cry and scream at the same time, like
Mozart's Requiem sung right. But he knows if
he takes it he'll have to give up everything.

And that's tough, because he's got a house
on the lake and a Honda Accord and he really
does still like the trout despite what I said,
and everything—EVERYTHING, DAMMIT, IS EVERYTHING.

Then one day he goes back, and the treasure—
well, I bet you didn't expect this—the treasure
is gone. His heart sinks—all the way down, below
the knees. "Shit happens." Sure it does, but you
can't blame this one on God. It was there, you
could have taken it, but you didn't. And now
he knows. It was the treasure made the house,
the car, the trout worthwhile. Without the treasure,
who cares? Without the treasure, where's the joy?
It's the treasure brings the joy. But we—we're
so dumb, we don't know that until it's gone.

The man in the parable, he was much smarter than
we are. He was onto something . . . very, very big.

What We Have

1.

Back roads curving through fields of cotton,
rough balls left by the pickers, brown tilled
soil still soft in the afternoon sun, sugar
maples screaming orange and red, tobacco smell
in weathered barns, children walking, packs
slung easy over shoulders, men talking
by roadside pumpkin stands.
                                              Sun slipping,
sand smooth on now bare feet, waves breaking
suddenly violet on the empty beach, ocean
glimmering gold as we stand, astonished,
at the moment's gift.
                                    Later we speak, touching
easily like cousins, bantering, bourbon in hand,
on the creekside dock as the moon rises, mirrored
in the still water.

2.

Morning on the river, birds circling, their nests
topping the marker poles. We turn down smaller
streams, then glide through arches made by spreading
oaks. No engine now, only the whir of line
and plop of lure, crookback minnow, purple worm,
flipped with the quick wrist under the twining vines.

3.

Night and the waves beat deep into the rhythm
of our dreams. Salt-tossed, we wake then sleep
again. I wake early, take the beach alone.
Willets, pipers gather for church, sleep through
bird sermon, one-legged, heads tucked under wings.
A solitary girl stares at the spray from the jetty's
end. I walk northward and wait for the sea to speak.

4.

Lingering, champagne in the noon sun, toes in sand,
we watch the ocean give us one last show. We hug
good-bye then see the reeds turn golden
in the creek. We leave before the sun, over
the bridge and into the orange woods. We speak
little. Our hearts devour what we have seen
and heard and smelt, pictures to thaw the winter
dark, what we have instead of God, instead of love.

Alphabet Soup

Alphabet Soup

Soon the words will mix like the jumbled
letters in alphabet soup sliding down
the throat finally to mingle in the stomach
with other things. Will it hurt, this loss?

Will I know, when it happens, that it is
happening? Today I tried to find the name
of someone, a man who coaches at my school.
He played basketball with Michael Jordan.

He is tall with slightly graying hair
and he bears the same name as some other
player, an even taller man. The one I know
is white, the other one is black.

At the game on Tuesday night a girl came up
and hugged me. I hugged her back. I asked her
how she was, and she presented me with her
beautiful four-year-old daughter. She took

classes with me, and acted in many plays.
Her name has slipped away.
It is like that now. Cells destructing
by the millions. Synapses sputtering.

Words like the jumbled letters of alphabet
soup, tumbling, tumbling down.

Wherever You Are

For Joan Edwards

That summer when I didn't write and I
rode blithely to Northport on the train
from New York, calling you at the station
to come and get me—as if nothing had
happened, as if we could resume, as if
the space between simply did not exist

You sent me back. I remember drinking
coffee in the station (you wouldn't even
take me to your house) and listening
to your voice, so self possessed and
absolutely right. I said nothing. What
could I say? "Forgive me, I'd like to
start again? I've been a fool? I love
you?" Not likely for a cool twenty
year-old from Princeton.

                    No he just took
the next train to the city and then
a week later wrote you from college
asking for his Ivy leaf back (now
buried somewhere on my wife's hockey
field in Norton, Massachusetts).

Then he was miserable for a whole year,
banging out his desperation on an Olivetti,
the hot typewriter of those times, hating
women, abandoning the whole business
of love, and why? Because he still loved
you and didn't know how to say it?
Because he was Ivy League, and scared
to say forgive me, I was wrong.

We might have been good together, you
and I. Your passion and my sense, your
love for art and mine for words. I
might have found the poet sooner than
I did.

Anyway, when I did learn
who I was, I searched for you at
Holyoke. I wanted to let you know
I was better, and could we be friends
now that I wasn't such a jerk. But
you were gone. No records, no forwarding
address. Forgive me, Joan.

The Last Day of Summer

On the last day of summer the sun sank slowly
through the roiling clouds into the surface
of the lake. It was evening, and for a moment
while the sun lay between clouds and water
the whole lake shone like burnished gold.

Afterwards, he stood on the dock and watched
the small brown leaves on the path to the house
and thought how soon the path itself would be
leaves. He thought of the goldfish, buried
for the winter in the covered pond and how

glad he had been to see them in the spring,
uncovered at Easter, safe for another year.
Now, his body bare, he glided into the smooth
lake and felt the warmth in his limbs for the final
time. In the morning they would leave

and when they came back another year
perhaps the quiet place where he had stood
and watched the orange sun come from under
the cloud and sink into the water would be changed
and he and the summer would be gone forever.

Unburdening

My books accuse me. They stare at me
in their various colored jackets from
the white shelves. They stare at me
from the stiff abandoned stacks between
the shelf and ceiling. They stare at me
from the floor. They are angry with me
because I do not love them as I once did.

The books with autographs frown at me
because I wish to put them up for adoption
at the local library. Homeless textbooks
from hungry publishers piled in corners
humbly request sanctuary. But I am cruel.
I am firm in my resolve, so much distracts
us from the task of being human.

I will keep the King James Bible my mother
gave me for my ninth Christmas. It is
the only thing I have that bears her name.
I will save *The Brothers Karamazov*, the poems
of Yeats and Rilke, a peacock feather from
Flannery O'Connor's farm, Andalusia,
her stories too, those dazzling stabs
of light that thrust us toward eternity.
I will keep the "Holy Sonnets" of John Donne
and certain gifts from friends whose
presence evokes mystery and awe. And letters . . .

From the file cabinets the letters murmur
to one another, the sounds of their voices
like the legs of cicadas in summer, thousands
in unison. The scribbled pleadings of Peter
Brewster from the Central Maine Hospital
for the Insane in 1963. The Gothic script
of my brother-in-law, Leonard Cowell Gordon,
now deceased, imploring me to intercede
on his behalf in my sister's divorce. The dark
straight lines of Corporal Joe Evans, my student
later killed in South Vietnam. The wide
smiling circles of my good angel, alfalfa
sprouts still sticking to the page.
Which ones shall I save?

Once You

Once you leaned over easily
and rubbing your hands in the dirt
anointed the bat
earth itself in the small cracks
of the Louisville slugger

once you saw the pitcher's
sudden wink
and the way the hand
came over his left ear
when he threw the curve

once you saw the seams
the rotation
the final slide
of the ball
as it dipped

and the bat as if by magic
sprung from its coil
arced beautifully
hips sprung
the ball a perfect line

and how you ran
oh, how you ran, circling
not so much a deer
but a dancer
a loping lovely dancer

once you stood
bowing at the end
the crowd like God's angels
blowing, blowing, blowing
until you raised your hand

for silence
to say goodbye
before it was all gone
and how glad I was
even with my tears

that you did not wait
for the slide into sadness
but said goodbye
to all of us
that day, standing

on home plate
your hat in your left hand
your right waving high
as if to tell us
never to be afraid

never to doubt
that we had seen
beauty and grace no one
even at the world's end
could take away

The Missing Heron

For Sara Beasley

In the long grass on the other bank, the heron
stands. If he sees me, my presence does not
disturb him. He does not fly, but if I moved,
say, or threw a stone in the smooth water
He would take wing.

           And so I speak to you
silently in my mind while I watch
the heron on the distant bank. You see, something
has happened. In my office, where the leaves glow
gold in the late October sun outside
my window, the students are strangely silent.
They speak only of their grades and the ways
           they can gain credit for their work abroad.

I know how long they wait outside your door
to watch you listen with that light behind
your eyes, how you smooth the jagged edges
of their wounds and sing them into life.

I only want what I cannot have, something back
which is lost like that last thrust of the October
sun through the yellow leaves, like the heron
who stood near the other bank when I began
these thoughts. I never saw him fly away
though I was looking toward him as I spoke.

Sarah's Laughter

For Laura Ann and Steven

Now Abraham and Sarah were old, advanced in age;
it had ceased to be with Sarah after the manner of women.
So Sarah laughed to herself, saying, "After I have grown old,
and my husband is old, shall I have pleasure?"

Genesis 18: 11-12

Praise to her laughter, and praise to the Lord
whose fingers planted the stars in the blue beds
of the night sky, whose mysteries are more strange
than the dark shapes in the green of the seas.

Praise to Sarah, who thought herself no longer
after the manner of women and laughed
that she should have joy in her autumn years,
And praise to Abraham, the father who waited

outside the tent in the heat of the dusky day
and smiled that he should be the bringer
of joy, that he should be once more, as they say,
after the manner of men. Praise to the Lord

for whom nothing is too hard. Should they not
dance and sing and stroke the silver
tambourine? Should they not cry for the gift
of love in the later years? Then Sarah said,

"God has made laughter for me," and Abraham
outside the tent smiled once more at the men
who rode through silken sands to bring
the news. And they would call his name, "Isaac,"

which means laughter, which means joy,
which means praise for the gift the Lord
has given.. "I did not laugh," Sarah said,
and the Lord answered, "No, but you did laugh."

Beyond the Ceiling of Our Dreams

To the memory of Michael deBurbure Turnure
and all those in the Class of 1957 who have gone before

God rests beyond the ceiling of our dreams
waiting somewhere to turn even the small hopes
of our lost loves into something beyond
the blue of our best imaginings. Listen!

Last year's swallow lies under the earth.
Death's sharp spade edges the red soil.

My friend, Michael, who stood so tall,
is gone now. My friend, Michael, who
could drive a thousand miles without blinking,
who walked into my wedding rehearsal in his
bright Hawaiian shirt and tight white pants,
Michael with his gorgeous tan who caused
my almost wife to blink and all the bridesmaids
to turn their slender necks, my friend Michael,
who brought me from boy to man and made me see
a world I never knew was there—is gone now.
Michael, who stood on the corner of Morris
Avenue and One Hundred and Sixty-Sixth Street
in cord jacket and grey flannel trousers, penny
loafers glowing in the sun of the south Bronx
while broken bottles splayed out in the gutters
beyond my sister's apartment. He had come
to drive me to college, come there in a car
to this street my other friends had never seen.

Michael is gone, who walked the steps
to Henry Tower every night of sophomore
year, who changed into clean shirts for dinner
and left the old ones lying on the floor until
the floor itself was shirts, Michael who smiled
at life and flew beyond the fields of my green
innocence, is gone. At the end, he sat
bolt upright in the bed and trumpeted
"Turnure" and then lay back down and smiled
that youthful smile one final time.

Beyond the ceiling of our dreams, God's fleshless
arms enclose him now, and all the others.

I speak their names with reverence. Fritz, I say,
whose class tie I wore at his daughter's wedding.
Milt, I say, and Tom, Rusty and Phil and Jerry.
Horsie, I say, Marty, Art and Wally. I say Dick
and Tod and Stu, Charlie and Larry and Peter—
some friends, some unknown, but we all walked
once with such light steps from Blair and Holder
to McCosh. How green, how green the grass then.

What we are given is short enough. Waters rise
and floods uproot the strongest trees. While
there is time, let us break bread together.
Let us follow the labyrinth to the secret center.
Above the shattered trees the stars still shine.

What the Mockingbird Said

A Poem for Elizabeth Chandler Cumming
on the occasion of her 90th Birthday

In the woods behind my house
under the white light of the full moon
a mocking bird sings and sings.
I know nothing about its song
or the way its tremulous notes
come from the throat, but I think,
as I hear the music in the dark,
of you—how you sing to us year
after year. The voice of our hopes,
the voice of our better selves—
the clear bell of conscience,
the deeper sound of simple duty.

When you speak, we know what is
right and why. You bring us the
wisdom of New England winters, and
the long trek of a marriage grown
richer by the soft fires of Carolina
nights, a marriage "better every
year" with the whirl of manuscripts
hidden in the walls of stony castles.

One day, on your sunny screened in
porch, we talked of shortened days
and living to the full, devouring
the marrow of each hour. You fooled
us all by clicking your heels at death
himself. And with that unexpected gift
of grace you built a life for all of us,
towers of compassion and rooms that hold
the fragile steps of the old in the tight
grip of love.

Time mocks us all, but you take the mock
and turn time's frown to laughter. The sun
shines in your window, where the red
amaryllis glows and glows. In the majesty
of your space and face, we are all kings.

The Slow Beginning of Our Lives

A meditation on turning sixty in the year 1995
For Bruce Rosborough

"The blues are a sixtyish burden. Once you strike
eighty though, you're suddenly young."
—Reynolds Price, *The Promise of Rest*

"An aged man is but a paltry thing
a tattered coat upon a stick, unless
Soul clap its hands and sing . . ."
—Yeats, *Sailing to Byzantium*

Act One: Spring

On Wednesday morning, April 19, the walls
of a bombed building in Oklahoma City peel
inward, folding the last of our illusions
into the sullen earth. A red-hatted firefighter
cradles year-old Baylee Almon. Their picture
graces our breakfast tables on Thursday:
How hard he hopes and with so little reason . . .

On Friday my college class reunes in the nation's
Capitol. At the embassies on Massachusetts Avenue
purses are checked for bombs. We mask our fears
with scotch and anecdotes, pictures of
grandchildren, tales of second wives
and lies passed down for forty years.
Our ears buzz. The words bounce off the walls.

Later, in the hotels, we watch again and again
the entrails hanging from what was once
a place where people worked and played.

On Saturday, in the art museum, we distract ourselves
with the masked courtesans of Venice and marvel
at how light shines on water. I wander
from the group and come upon the faces
of Vermeer, those women who look up at us
surprised to see them reading. If there were
no guards I would touch those eyes
and the high cheek bones of da Vinci's

Genevra de' Benci in the adjoining room.
For a time the sadness leaves, but in
the afternoon it comes again in the cowed
darkness of cattle cars. Piles of hair and teeth
and shoes and the grim faced negligence of guards
remind us how—when we were only ten—the world
made charred bones of its soul.

Act Two: Summer

In July the woods of Bosnia burn.
Muslims die by thousands in unmarked graves.
Towns whose names we can't pronounce—Nova
Kasaba, Srebrenica—hold the holy blood
of martyrs. A farmer named Hurem Suljic
plays dead by the side of the road, bodies
piled on top of his to hide his breathing.
He lives to tell the story.

August now, and Hurricane Felix stalls off
the Carolina coast, teasing the shore with gusts
of ninety miles. It edges northward
toward Virginia, its force diminished. Mickey
Mantle is dead of cancer at sixty-three, and
The Simpson trial is still savage farce. About
Bosnia the press is strangely quiet.

Act Three: Autumn

Tuesday, October 3, and the Simpson trial
has ended. At one p.m. Eastern Daylight Time
the world stopped. On the campus of Augustana
College in Rock Island, Illinois, students
gathered, black and white together, to listen
to the verdict. On the cover of *Newsweek*
a photographer has captured their response—
blacks clapping, slapping high fives,
mouths open with song.

Whites sit pale, faceless, thin
lips tight in silence. Kim Goldman weeps
on the television set. It is the same everywhere.

Act Four: Winter

The world whirls downward into darkness.
Snow sheets the midwest. Eastern cities
cease, sculptured in ice. Vermeer is closed,
streets empty, houses abandoned in the Maryland
suburbs. Newt and the President wrangle.

In The Everglades old friends meet to ease
the pain of loss. The sun shines, and the only
words we hear are the names of birds—snowy heron
and ibis, egret, the snakelike black anhinga.
The roseate spoonbill shocks us with a rush
of pink and white.

It is New Year's Day, and our canoes cut
silently though the dark water. The tourists
are blessedly few, many trapped at home
by the icy wings of the winter storm. We paddle
slowly, our muscles sore from lack of use.

We wonder who we are, on this day, at this
slow beginning of our lives—widows,
retirees, strangers to the world of play
and contemplation.

On the third morning we rise in blackness
and watch the sun slip from the eastern sea.
The birds take wing toward the Gulf.
In our canoes, we sit silent, as if at the dawn
of time. Here there are no rumbling trains,
no walls falling. It will be better now. It must.

Act Five: Spring

The year circles on itself. Peace of a sort
in Bosnia, and in Oklahoma City mothers and sons,
sisters and friends gather to mourn.
Spring is brief and slow. In Minnesota the lilac
does not bloom till June, and on Southern campuses
old grads are dismayed by dogwood and azaleas
a month delayed. But spring it is, and I think
here on my screened porch—if I could remember
the name of that extraordinary flower climbing
my neighbor's mailbox, twining itself round
and round, like a white snake in Eden, if I could
hear the hummingbird sucking the sweet water
or see the pair of cardinals eating the seed
at the feeder, then isn't that enough? It is still
spring, however slow.

Epilogue: 1997

On Father's Day, Tara Hope Burr is born
in the front seat of her parents' Jeep
Cherokee on the way to the hospital in Monroe,
North Carolina. Her grandmother, a nursing
student, sitting in the back seat, pats
the baby's back to let her breathe. Tara
lets out a scream, and so they arrive—
baby, mother, father, and grandma—
at the emergency room door. The next day
in black T-shirt and Braves baseball cap
the father shaves in the family's room.
On the bed behind, the mother
cradles the child.

Sunset on Skiff Mountain

Sunset on Skiff Mountain, and the snow
silent and white as a bride's veil.
Wednesday afternoons in winter I drive
the winding road from the shadowed valley
and marvel at the moment the sun breaks
through the arms of the sleeveless trees,
marvel how in this hour before dark
light is restored like Joseph to his brothers
in Egypt after the long lean years. I stand
by the pond in the fallow fields in utter
gratitude. Something here is given,
some grace we never had to earn.

If I died tonight I would take this
with me, like the letter O. O, I would say,
And O and O and O again.

The sun lowering and the distant hills
like slumbering giants, beckoning—
beckoning.

The Search for Wonder
in the Cradle of the World

That Which Cannot Be Done

A Yank, a Frenchman, and a Japanese
    learning German at the Goethe Institute
        meet a learned Turk on the train to Berlin.

"Ah," says the Turk, "then you must see
    the beautiful Altar of Zeus
        from Ancient Pergamum the Germans

stole from us so many years ago.
    I will take you myself." At the thought
        his eyes shine like pearls.

Before the Altar in the State Museum
    beyond the bounds of Checkpoint Charlie
        the Turk weeps. The Frenchman, the Yank

and the Japanese are shamed by such excess
    but the Turk does not care.
        "It is so beautiful," he sighs

knowing as they do not how a German
    entrepreneur had shipped the Altar
        piece by piece in the black of night

to hired boats. The Turks never knew
    what he had done until the priceless
        stones were well beyond their grasp.

At the exit door the Turk stops
    and weeps again, then turns
        to the ancient guardian ladies

in their threadbare uniforms
    and asks to go back in.
        "Nein," the ladies answer,

"Der ausgang ist kein eingang.
    This thing cannot be done."
        But the Turk is passionate.

"It is so beautiful," he cries.
     "You have stolen this work of art
          from my people." He begs

to go back in. "Nein," the ladies
     say once more, and again
          the Turk weeps to see such beauty

snatched from Turkish shores.
     The guardians weaken. "Yes,"
          one says, "It is so beautiful.

But in your country you have
     so many beautiful things.
          We have so few, so few.

Go in der ausgang, go in and see
     this beautiful thing again."
          And she too weeps to see

the Turk pass by the exit door
     to see once more the beautiful
          Altar of Zeus from Pergamum.

Foreign Service

For Nursel

In the fields white-veiled women work
beside the men. At lunch they gather separately
to talk. In village squares black-coated rooster
males strut in threes and fours, while scarfed
mothers, left at home, play soccer with their sons,
sliding awkwardly down the slow fields
in their heavy skirts.

                We watch from the bus,
our tongues tied by the banalities of travel
in a foreign land. We are limited to nouns
and simple expletives. Verbs and adjectives
lie far beyond our baby tongues. "Tuvalet,"
we say, for "toilet," and "hayir" for "no."
"Gunaydin" for "good morning" exceeds our Texans'
reach. "Tesekkur" for "thank you" is like
the terrible twelfth grade.

                Nursel, our guide,
is as gentle as last night's rain. She tells us
of the Hittites and the Seljuk Turks, the Phrygians
and the troglodytes who burrowed in the earth
like moles. Even the Texans listen. She mispronounces
"v's" so sweetly we wish the way she speaks the words
were right. "Wisit," she says, as we approach
the "walley" of Goreme.

                She teaches at the university,
takes tours between semesters to see her through.
She speaks softly but with passion of her poems and her
love for all people. She tells me of the lovers
from St. Louis, one white, one black, she took through
Cappadocia last year. She will serve one day in her
country's foreign service, if she passes her exams.

Nursel, my sweet Caucasian friend, go well. The dead
in Sarajevo, the wounded in New York, cry out for you.

Walking on Water

On the waterside in Tiberias, the city
the Romans made, bearded peddlers hawk
golden "feesh, two for a dollar."

Pilgrims board boats for Capernaum,
billed as "the home town of Jesus"
in the slick magazines, a thirty-minute

ride north on a nice day, though
the Sea of Galilee, as we all know,
is prone to sudden storms, especially

in early spring. On the upper deck
the captain sells sea-shell bracelets
made by sailors' wives. Below, pilgrims

sing hymns they know by heart. When
the wind comes up, I'm standing
at the rail musing on how Jesus walked

across the lake and the disciples
scared in their small boat. We huddle
below with the pilgrims to escape

the rain, watching their mouths move
with words that make no sense to us,
watching their lean pale faces and .

the crutches of the lame who'll walk
the hill outside of town to the Mount
of the Beatitudes and be blessed

by the priests. Later, in Capernaum
peddlers hawk postcards, "two for a dollar"
at the synagogue where Jesus taught

as a child. Multitudes gather. Multitudes
walk the hill to the place where Jesus
stood and spoke the Sermon on the Mount.

I stand amazed, mouth open, to see
so many here. The field is full of folk
and flowers. The lame lie down in the long

grass, and Jesus speaks to them. From
over the water he comes and stands
and speaks. Down below the buses belch

diesel smoke and wait.

Running the Gauntlet

In Egypt you bargain for everything
    from postcards to papyrus
        from sacred beetles to bracelets.

"Bekam?," (how much) you ask, slyly,
    pretending cool, but watching
        the boys in their green galabiyas

lest they get too close, close enough
    to put their hands on you
        close enough to say, "Lady . . .

I like you." They want you inside
    off the street, beyond the eyes
        of the others who would draw you away

with a better color, a smaller price
    a cousin in Philadelphia named Ahmed
        a smile and an honest seeming eye,

It's rough out there, these men with sticks
    beating you—no smacking each other
        day after day after bloody day.

One guy cried, actually cried, said
    his family was starving, had sold nothing
        for fifteen days. The terrorists

had kept the trade away. Business was bad.
    Sometimes you stay on the boat or bus
        just to rest. Still they pound windows

And smile from the dusty street.
    When you feel good, you come out armed,
        laughing with what you've learned.

"How much?"you ask. "Twenty Egyptian pounds,"
    the man says, holding out the cotton shawl.
        "Mushma'ool!" you shout,

"Unbelievable!" He laughs, and brings the price
to ten. "Two," you say. At the end
you buy it for five. You didn't want

it anyway, but once you start, you can't
back off and walk away. Then they grab
you in earnest. Then you're in

another game altogether.

Nile Journey

The sky, a cloudless blue, speaks
of peace, and the river bears us slowly
to a simpler time. Black haired boys

in galabiyas prod donkeys along the banks,
while water buffaloes pull plows
through fields of sugar cane. Time stops.

But for all the miles the sun still sets
each night in the west and the soul
searches stars of a different color.

In their vast impotence the monuments
echo death, buried and resurrected
for the stares of multitudes. We gawk

at gods with heads of cows, with beaks
of hawks or the faces of crocodiles.
We wonder what hold they had on the faithful.

On the wall of a tomb, the artist
has depicted the journey of a young prince
to the underworld. The blues of three

millenia shine as if painted yesterday.
His father introduces him to Osiris,
God of the dead, and to falcon-headed

Horus, as if to old friends. Protect
him well, the father says. He is too
young to journey by himself. We would

ask no more. But pictures are only
wishes, and all the images on all the tombs
stand silent at the foot of truth's dark tower

whose winding stairs we climb and climb
again, past the Pharaohs' silly boats,
their amulets and cunningly wrought chains

into the grasp of the fleshless hands of God.

Oedipus: at the Place Where Three Roads Meet

At the place where three roads meet
Oedipus stops. He has walked from Delphi,
he has walked up the Sacred Way
from the gurgling spring to the space
where the Sybil waits with answers
to the questions of our lives.

Now he knows, now he has heard
her words, and he turns toward Corinth—
no, toward Thebes—to charm his fate
to death, to laugh his destiny
into the black hole where snakes
of superstition dwell. He will smile
at the Sphinx, scoff at the old man
who blocks his way, and place his tongue
in the mouth of the woman he loves.

He will be king. He will give laws.

At the place where three roads meet
he looks down the road to Thebes
and does not see the silver brooches
from his mother's gown tearing, tearing
at the circles of his all knowing eyes.

Behind him, on Parnassus, wild flowers
bloom, and the muses weep silently.

Dodona: Sunday Morning

It is Sunday morning, and I am sitting alone
on the stone steps of the theatre of Dodona.
It is Sunday morning, and to the east the rays
of the sun touch the sacred ground of the oracle
of Zeus. It is a Sunday morning in April
and wild flowers, red and yellow, have begun
to bloom in the wet grass. To the south the high
peaks of the Pindus range are white from last
night's snow. It is April, and the flowers
are blooming, yet the high mountains are white.

The voice of Zeus rolled once from these hills
through the mouths of the sibyls. The drunken
mouths of the sibyls who had breathed the fumes
of the sacred springs. Those who sat on these steps
saw his eagle circling over the distant snow-capped
hills. Now it is Sunday morning, and I have climbed
over the tourist gate to sit here alone while
the April sun rises over the eastern ridge.

The ticket office is closed, the buses have departed,
and the first taxis of the day have not yet made
the winding drive from the valley below. No sign
of life except my footprints in the dew, and the
sun slanting through ancient columns, and the eagle
of Zeus soaring from the snow-capped hills. It is
Sunday morning and I am sitting, alone, on the stone
steps of the theatre of Dodona near the oracle of Zeus.

From the Balcony of the Grand Bretagne

It is Sunday and the streets of Athens
are empty, the stores closed and barred.
From the balcony of the Grand Bretagne
I can see the broken roof of the Parthenon,
the scaffolding, the giant yellow crane
which too is silent in deference to the day

Or should I say the gods? I do not know.
For days I have walked in search of them—
smelled the incense in the night, blinked
at candles, groped in alleys for the elusive
moment—caught like the others the pull
of the heart before the porch of the caryatids.

I have looked for signs of their presence
in the grass that grows between the broken
stones by the Temple of Athene Nike, sat
upon the Areopagus gazing up the high stairs
trying to decipher the cryptic codes of the
strange letters carved in the slippery rock.

And now it is Sunday and the streets are
empty, the temples closed, and I can only
sit on my balcony at the Grand Bretagne
and watch the broken roof, the scaffolding,
the giant yellow crane. With my right hand
I click the stones in my pocket. With my left

I cover my eyes and pray for the parthenos,
the maiden of the stony hill, to restore my sight.

Under the Marble's Chiseled Skin

To the Memory of Robert A. Ward

In the last great Pieta of Michelangelo
the body of the dead Christ drags Mary
downward into the grave itself, drags
all of us with its stark and awful weight
downward into the grave itself. His left
arm, twisted by the wracking cross, bends
almost backward, the broken wrist thrust
outward mockingly into our quiet space.

The good always go first. Not even the love
of God can save them. Christ's neck
is broken. His head lies heavy on his
mother's invisible cheek. The good always
go first, not fading away like that old soldier
you loved so much, but like the Christ
of Michelangelo, heavy, heavy into the grave.

We look again at the sculpture. Our eyes
lift upward to the head above Christ's.
It is Joseph of Arimathea, the old man
who has given his own tomb to Jesus.
He does not mourn for the death of his
friend, nor does he turn away in scorn.
But his wise eyes are bright with some
knowledge only he and the sculptor share.
His wise eyes glow with understanding.

As I stand here looking into this lovely
face I think of you and wish you here
with me, standing with your wise bright eyes
next to me, telling me what you see
under the marble's chiseled skin. We miss
your wisdom and the quiet wit that drew
us to you long before your days of fame.
Father, we called you, half in jest and half
in reverence. I think you knew what Joseph
of Arimathea knew looking downward at the
broken body of his friend. You knew the place
where the soul lies, the place where the soul
flies, and that the tomb is but a door
into the welcome, radiant smile of God.

This Monster Time

From Masaccio's "Expulsion"

This is the moment time begins.
Before—nothing but playing in the
dimpled shade—some milk and honey
dream of endless love. Now there is time.

No one had quite caught it in paint
like Ugly Tom, who must have felt
himself the pain and seen it on
the faces of his friends. Nothing

ideal here. No nudes here. Nothing
gentle or genteel. Just nakedness,
pure nakedness forked out before us.
And the horror in Eve's eyes of the

history that will start unreeling
here forever—Dresden, Auschwitz,
Hiroshima. Adam's guilt hidden
in his hands. Better not to see.

I thought once Eve was modest, now
I know she's only cold and sick, sick
of what they've made and unmade.
Sick at the gurgle of blood in her

son's throat and husband's too,
sick at the sight of her distant
daughters on the road to Beirut
chilled in their black chadours.

Time begins here with these steps,
Adam's right leg dragging at the gate,
Eve's belly swelling. This night
they will sleep in some hollow

and chew on reeds. He will hold her
in his arms, but their eyes will
never meet and they will wonder how
this unravelling began—this monster time.

Pieta

The dead in their long sleeves reach to us
from their littered past. Driving down
a rural Southern highway, I almost leave
the road thinking of how the face of Jesus
in Michelangelo's early Pieta is that
of my father. His neck rests on Mary's arm.
His hand hangs down into the folds
of her robe. The dark nail hole cuts
between his veins. But he feels nothing.
He is at peace. Oh, how the Christ shines,
how his limbs glow with the sculptor's love.

When I stood at St. Peter's my nosed pressed
to the glass like a schoolboy at the aquarium
I did not know this. I did not see my father's
face or the face of my sister Elizabeth
in Mary's. But it is she, so young,
with so many years to live now without him.
He is at peace, with his thin beard and his
long, graceful feet. But she mourns still
today silently under the folds of her heavy robe.

Come Lord Jesus

From Bernini, "The Ecstasy of St. Teresa"

At the Piazza della Republica I see the gypsy
girls, one coming at me from the front with the
big sheet of cardboard, the other circling behind.
"Fuck off," I say in Italian, having had the trick
described to me. I cross away from them, looking
for the Largo San Susanna, looking for the Church
of Santa Maria della Vittoria. No one has heard
of it. I have come to see "The Ecstasy
of St. Teresa," but no one knows where it is.

I stand at the top of Via Barberini, showing
my paper to passers by. They shake their heads
and go. Go home, they seem to say, don't worry.
But I do. I have seen the slides in art class
and felt my breath catch even at the pictures.
I have carried the paper with the name of the place
written in Italian so all can understand.
This is my day to see Bernini's "Ecstasy."

I find it by checking churches. There are
four within the block, and the one I seek's
the last of course, covered in scaffolding
and offering nothing at the door except
an invitation to darkness inside, the usual
candles and second-rate baroque. No wonder
the guide books leave it out, I think. And then
I catch it with the corner of my eye and pray
to be alone awhile to let it play on me.

Wherever she is going, she is already there.
"Come Lord Jesus," she says with her open mouth.
Her lidded eyes have slowly closed. Her hand
with its delicate long fingers hangs limply
from the rock where she lies. Her foot falls
loosely into our space. She is one with God.
"Come, Lord Jesus" she has said, and we know
at once the angel is superfluous, the silly
smiling angel, his spear about to pierce
her heart. She has traveled far beyond

his thrust and the leering eyes of the
carved nobles in the boxes on either side
who gaze at her erotically. They cannot find
her. I don't know what the angel thinks.
He's just a boy who's never used a spear
like this before. What I'd like, though,
is the angel's view. He sees her whole
as I cannot, bound to earth as I am.

Later, the schoolgirls come, giggling
while their teacher talks, whispering
to one another of some obscenity they see.
I close my book and leave by the other
aisle. On the street outside the gypsies
ply their trade in the late summer sun.

Anthony S. Abbott was born in San Francisco. He was educated at Princeton and Harvard and is Charles A. Dana Professor of English at Davidson College.

His poems have appeared in *New England Review, Southern Poetry Review, St. Andrews Review, Pembroke, Tar River Poetry, Theology Today, Anglican Theological Review,* and many others. His first book of poetry, *The Girl in the Yellow Raincoat,* was published by St. Andrews College Press in 1989 and nominated for the Pulitzer Prize. His second collection, *A Small Thing Like a Breath,* was published by St. Andrews in 1993.

He lives in Davidson, North Carolina with his wife Susan. They have three sons and six grandchildren.